CARSON WENTZ

SOARING
WITH THE
EAGLES

TURRON DAVENPORT

TRIUMPH
BOOKS

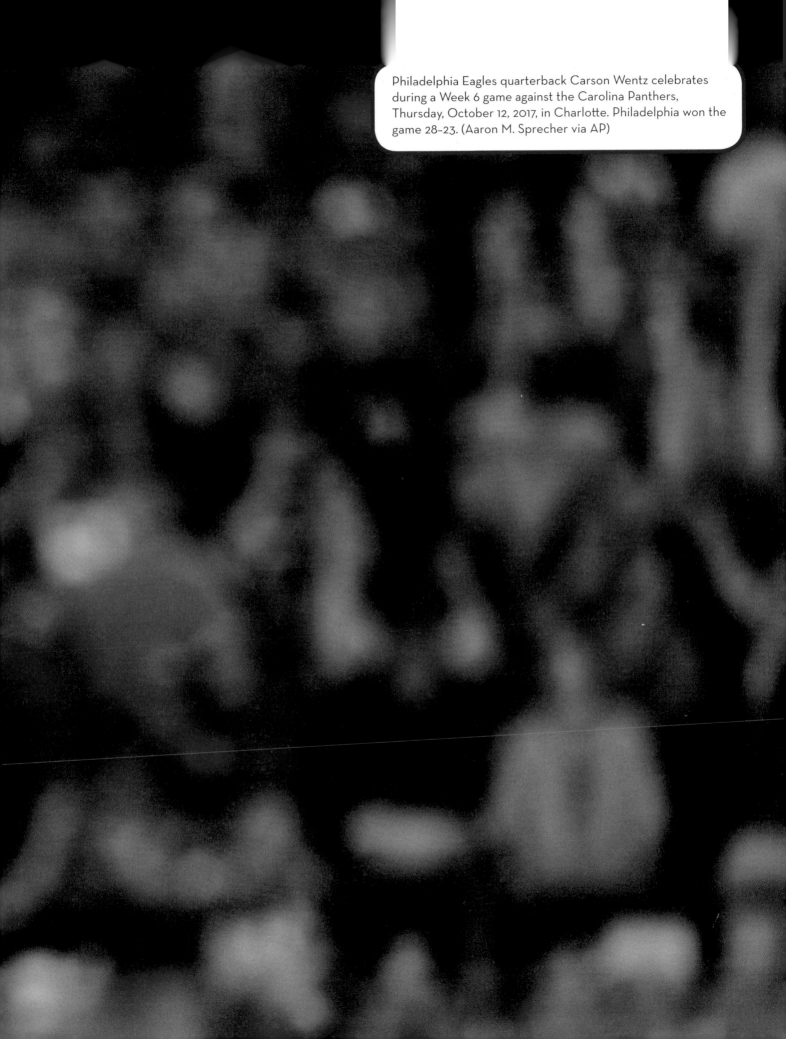

Philadelphia Eagles quarterback Carson Wentz celebrates during a Week 6 game against the Carolina Panthers, Thursday, October 12, 2017, in Charlotte. Philadelphia won the game 28–23. (Aaron M. Sprecher via AP)

This book is available in quantity at special discounts
for your group or organization.
For further information, contact:

Triumph Books LLC
814 North Franklin Street
Chicago, Illinois 60610
Phone: (312) 337-0747
www.triumphbooks.com

Printed in U.S.A.
ISBN: 978-1-62937-593-9

Interior Design: Patricia Frey
Cover Design: Andy Hansen

AP Images

Contents

North Dakota's Native Son

Carson Wentz's rise to NFL stardom is as rapid as the growth spurt that he experienced while he was at Century High School in Bismarck, North Dakota. He went from a 5-foot-8 freshman to a 6-foot-5 star senior quarterback.

He played baseball, basketball, and football in high school. As a junior, Wentz did not play basketball so he could concentrate on football. He played basketball once again during his senior year and helped Century win a state championship.

Shoulder and arm problems caused Wentz to play wide receiver as a junior. The shoulder injury came from playing baseball, where he was a three-year starter playing first base.

Wentz used to gather some of his receivers and sneak into the Community Bowl in Bismark and have them run routes for him. He would pick them up in his old 2004 gold Nissan Frontier and drive to an adjacent lot so they could sneak into the stadium and play catch for hours.

On the football field, Wentz was the 2010 North Dakota Class 3A Player of the Year. The all-conference quarterback and defensive back led Century to an 8–3 record and a state semifinals appearance in 2010.

Century High School isn't only known for producing one of the NFL's fastest rising stars. The high school was also attended by 2017 Miss America Cara Mund, along with Wentz.

She mentioned her classmate in her acceptance speech.

"I said, 'If Carson Wentz can do it, Miss North Dakota Cara Mund can become Miss America.'"

Becoming a Bison

Wentz didn't receive a single Division I scholarship offer despite a stellar career at

North Dakota State quarterback Carson Wentz (11) tries to break a tackle by Iowa State linebacker Jared Brackens (14) during the second half, Saturday, August 30, 2014, in Ames, Iowa. North Dakota State won 34-14. (AP Photo/Charlie Neibergall)

Century High. The decision to stay in the state and become a member of the North Dakota State Bison football team was a no-brainer. Although he played a different sport, Wentz just followed his brother's footsteps.

Wentz's brother Zach was a four-year starting pitcher and infielder for North Dakota State's baseball team. Zach set career records for games played, hits, and doubles. He was a vital part of a 40-win team in 2012.

Playing sports at North Dakota State is a part of life for the Wentz family. His cousin, Connor, was a tight end on his 2013, 2014, and 2015 football teams at North Dakota State.

The Bison won their first FCS championship in Wentz's freshman year. Wentz didn't have a real hand in the team's championship, but the winning habits that he now shows on Sundays grew from seeds that were planted at North Dakota State.

Wentz backed up quarterback Brock Jensen as a redshirt freshman. He threw his first touchdown pass against Prairie View A&M when he was able to enter the game in relief of Jensen. Wentz was a perfect 8-for-8 in that game and finished the day with 93 passing yards in addition to his touchdown throw.

He would have to wait another season to be the starter, as Jensen held onto the job as a senior in 2013. Wentz's best game that season was against Delaware State. He completed 10-of-13 attempted passes for 105 passing yards and a touchdown.

Wentz celebrates with his team after scoring the go-ahead touchdown against Illinois State during the FCS championship game, Saturday, January 10, 2015, in Frisco, Texas. North Dakota State won the game 29–27 for their fourth straight national championship. (AP Photo/Tim Sharp)

Carrying on the Championship Tradition

Once 2014 rolled around, it was Wentz's turn to take over under center. The responsibility of carrying on the winning tradition for the Bison was placed squarely on Wentz's shoulders.

Their first task was playing against Iowa State, a heavily favored FBS opponent. Wentz was able to efficiently rise to the occasion and come out on top by completing 18-of-28 pass attempts for 204 yards in a 34–14 victory.

Wentz led NDSU to a 15–1 record in his first season as a starting quarterback. He started all 16 games in 2014, completing 228-of-358 passes for 3,111 yards with 25 touchdowns and 10 interceptions.

Oh, and, for good measure, Wentz was the Bison's second-leading rusher, with 642 rushing yards and six rushing touchdowns. North Dakota State's leading rusher John Crockett went on to the NFL the next season.

Wentz capped off his junior season with a spectacular performance in the national championship game against Illinois State. He finished the day with 287 yards passing and a touchdown. He also rushed for 87 yards in the win. One of his carries was a five-yard run to give North Dakota State the lead with 37 seconds left in the game. The defense held on to secure a 29–27 win and give the Bison their fourth consecutive national championship.

It was during his fifth year at North Dakota State when things got tough. Wentz had a career game against Northern Iowa when he passed

Wentz accepts the trophy for the most valuable player after the FCS championship game, Saturday, January 9, 2016, in Frisco, Texas. North Dakota State beat Jacksonville State 37-10 to win their fifth consecutive championship. (AP Photo/Mike Stone)

for a career-high 335 yards. The very next week, Wentz suffered a broken wrist, but still managed to finish the game!

The Bison lost to South Dakota, and Wentz was out for the next eight weeks. But he didn't let the injury keep him from having an impact on his team's success.

Wentz worked extensively in the classroom with redshirt freshman quarterback Easton Stick. Wentz was a mentor to Stick just as Jensen had been to him a couple of years earlier.

North Dakota State went on to win the next seven games and earn another shot at the national championship. Wentz returned to practice in December and started the national championship game against Jacksonville State.

His two rushing touchdowns and a passing touchdown fueled the Bison to their fifth consecutive national title.

Leaving a Legacy

Wentz is only the 52nd NFL player from the state of North Dakota, and only the third from Bismarck. Even though other players have gone on to the NFL from North Dakota State, none took the state by storm the way Wentz did.

North Dakota is Minnesota Vikings and Green Bay Packers territory, but now there are just as many people who watch Wentz's Philadelphia Eagles at Bismarck sports bars on Sundays.

The way the people of North Dakota adopted Wentz as their native son was evident when Eagles head coach Doug Pederson, GM Howie Roseman, and team owner Jeffrey Lurie went there to meet with him at dinner.

Roseman was astonished by the reactions from people when Wentz entered the restaurant.

"He walks into the restaurant, just the impressions people have. It was an interesting moment because we walked into the restaurant and I had to step out for a second," Roseman said during his press conference after selecting Wentz in the NFL Draft. "When I walked back in, I saw the manager and the hostess talking to each other and saying, 'Carson is just the greatest guy. He's always so humble, and he's always so appreciative of all of us here.' They didn't know what we were doing, and it was just— that's the kind of kid he is."

One family traveled more than 1,500 miles from Jamestown, North Dakota, to South Philadelphia to see their favorite player. Chuck and Karen Anderson have been rooting for Wentz since his days at North Dakota State. They wanted to see him in person at Eagles training camp during the summer.

"It's just awesome to be included in all this stuff. It's just great. I get the dream. Once in a lifetime, maybe," Chuck Anderson said to Channel 6ABC.

"He's awesome. Such a role model for our kids and grandkids," Karen Anderson said as she tried to keep from crying. "Just being here, being away from North Dakota, to get to be here. It's just great."

In addition to the green and yellow Bison colors, fans have taken to the Eagles' green and gray like proud parents solely because it's the second home of their adopted son. ★

Wentz is congratulated by fans following the FCS championship game against Illinois State, Saturday, January 10, 2015, in Frisco, Texas. (AP Photo/Tim Sharp)

Wentz works out with the North team during practice for the Senior Bowl, Wednesday, January 27, 2016, at Ladd-Peebles Stadium, in Mobil, Alabama. (AP Photo/Brynn Anderson)

Rapid Rise Before the Draft

The meteoric rise that Carson Wentz made before the 2016 NFL Draft was unprecedented. He went from a little-known FCS quarterback at the beginning of the year to what many viewed as the best quarterback in the country.

The hype train really got rolling just before Wentz traveled to Mobile, Alabama, for the Senior Bowl. NFL Network draft analyst Mike Mayock pointed to Wentz as a player to watch as Senior Bowl week approached.

It all started when Mayock was doing some film prep for the players he was going to see at the Senior Bowl.

"The way I look at Wentz, the first tape I put in, I went 'Wow.' I didn't even know who he was. He was just a quarterback on my list," Mayock said. "I watched this big kid sling the ball around a lot, and on top of it, was athletic enough that they planned quarterback runs for him.

"So you do some homework, and you find out he's 6-5, 235. And I put the second tape in hoping it would be as good as the first—and it was better. So you start doing homework on the kid, and yeah, he's only got 23 starts, but he's 20–3 as a starter at a great program in Division I-AA, [with] five consecutive national championships."

Senior Bowl Standout

Mayock's opinion only got stronger after watching him for a week of practice.

"When I look at him, I see a kid that's as athletic or more athletic than Andrew Luck," Mayock said, via Mary Kay Cabot of the *Cleveland Plain Dealer.* "He's bigger than Andrew Luck. He's got arm strength comparable to Andrew Luck. He just doesn't have the experience that Andrew Luck had at a high level that Andrew had coming out of college. So I see a ceiling for this kid

Wentz works out during his pro day, Thursday, March 24, 2016, in Fargo, North Dakota. (AP Photo/Bruce Crummy)

similar to Andrew Luck. That's why I believe in this kid so much. But it's going to take a little bit of time."

NFL scouts and evaluators learned a lot about Wentz when they saw him in person during the week of practices leading up to the Senior Bowl. Many were enamored with his big frame and the athleticism that he showed. It was the big arm that he displayed that really caught the attention of the scouts.

By the time the week of practice was over, Wentz was named the starter for the North team in the Senior Bowl game. He came out and completed his first pass, a three-yard completion to tight end Nick Vaannett on the first play of the game.

Wentz finished the game having completed 6-of-10 pass attempts for 50 yards. The impression was made by Wentz during that week. The momentum officially hit overdrive.

The Dallas Cowboys coaching staff coached Wentz and the North team during the week. Former NFL quarterback turned Cowboys head coach Jason Garrett enjoy working with Wentz. He came away extremely impressed with him.

"He responded very well," Garrett said of Wentz, per Pro Football Talk. "When he went against the guys at the Senior Bowl, I thought he fit in really well. He's a small-school guy, but he's a very impressive guy as an individual, just the way he carries himself, his leadership. He's very impressive physically. He's a big kid, athletic, and he can throw the football. It was a good week for us to get to know him."

Wentz runs the 40-yard dash drill at the NFL Combine, Saturday, February 27, 2016, in Indianapolis. (AP Photo/ Darron Cummings)

Crushing the Combine

Next for Wentz came the NFL Combine. His formal interview with the Philadelphia Eagles blew the team away. Quarterbacks coach John DeFilippo asked Wentz how he feels about some of the people who say he will struggle to make the jump from North Dakota State to the NFL.

"It is what it is. Those things are out of my control. It's all in the past, but I believe I made the most of my opportunities and then some," Wentz responded. "If anyone wants to doubt that, I am more than ready to prove them wrong. That's my attitude, and I am just ready to roll."

The answer impressed the Eagles brass that included GM Howie Roseman, head coach Doug Pederson, offensive coordinator Frank Reich, and team owner Jeffrey Lurie. That's quite a group to have your first interview with!

Wentz aced the test and impressed everyone as they talked pass protection, play concepts, and more. The Eagles were convinced they had to have him, but only had the 13th overall pick. With the Dallas Cowboys holding the No. 4 overall pick and their interest in Wentz being no secret, it was clear the Eagles needed to jump ahead of Dallas if they wanted to get him.

Wentz excelled during Combine workouts as he displayed his big arm by putting throws on the money from the hash to the sideline on out-breaking routes by the receivers. That's a pro level throw that separates the good from the great quarterbacks, and Wentz consistently completed it with ease.

He showed some touch on deep passes, but the one area that continued to be an issue was his accuracy on deeper crossing routes. Nevertheless, the Combine was another rung on the ladder toward the top of the draft.

As he continued to rise, Wentz showed the confidence that is fitting for a franchise quarterback.

"I am not sure how it happened. But I have been in total control of what I can control and focused on that," Wentz said on NFL Network. "Am I surprised? Not really. I kind of expected this and hoped for it. It was a goal. We are not done and have a lot of work to do. I am looking forward to hearing my name called at the draft in April."

Passing on Pro Day

Wentz held his pro day workout at the Fargo Dome in North Dakota in late March of 2016. The weather conditions created flight delays for some NFL franchises that attempted to send representatives to the workout.

There were 14 NFL teams represented at Wentz's pro day. That pales in comparison to the 32 teams that attended fellow top prospect Jared Goff's pro day.

Cleveland Browns head coach Hue Jackson was one of the higher-ranking personnel people in attendance—in fact, he was the only head coach there! The Browns held the No. 2 overall pick at the time.

With Cleveland being a city notorious for severe weather, Browns assistant coach Pep Hamilton conducted the workout. They doused the football with water to simulate poor throwing conditions.

Although he played in North Dakota, Wentz and the Bison had the benefit of

Philadelphia Eagles head coach Doug Pederson speaks during a press conference at the NFL Combine in Indianapolis, February 24, 2016. (AP Photo/Michael Conroy, File)

playing their home games indoors. But the challenge of throwing a wet football didn't rattle Wentz, even after his first pass slipped out of his hands and torpedoed into the turf.

"I just had to get used to the first one, and obviously it went right into the dirt. But I got the feel for it after that, and I thought it was all right." Wentz said on NFL Network. "I mean, it happens. Anytime you're playing with a wet football, it's not going to be perfect. It was pretty doused. That would've been torrential downpour there. I thought it was all right."

According to NFL Media senior analyst Gil Brandt, Wentz completed 63-of-65 passes during the workout, one of which was dropped. Brandt called it one of the best pro day workouts he had ever seen and said Wentz reminded him of Baltimore Ravens quarterback Joe Flacco.

Pepperoni or Sausage? Vanilla or Chocolate?

Eagles head coach Doug Pederson saw both University of California quarterback Jared Goff and Wentz in person. He put each of them through a pre-draft workout but seemed to be leaning toward Wentz.

"Carson is a bit of a better athlete right now. He is bigger, more mobile, but both of them have a chance to be franchise quarterbacks. At 218 pounds, Goff is probably the more undersized of the two," Pederson said during a pre-draft press conference. "I played at 218 pounds as well so I don't put a lot into weight. They are very similar but have different strengths and weaknesses. I liked working them out and getting my hands on them."

GM Howie Roseman coined his infamous "pepperoni or sausage" phrase when he was asked about being able to take one of the top two quarterbacks in the draft.

"We're very sure we're going to get the player we want," Roseman said. "It's like vanilla or chocolate, you know? It's like pepperoni pizza or sausage. What do you like better?"

Making a Move for Their Man

The Eagles were convinced that Wentz was their guy. The only thing they had to figure out was how to get into the position to select him.

Unlike many others in the draft community, Cleveland did not think Wentz would develop into a franchise quarterback. Roseman was able to negotiate a deal with the Browns allowing Philadelphia to move up to the No. 2 overall pick.

The Los Angeles Rams had already acquired the No. 1 overall pick in the draft from the Tennessee Titans. Tennessee was in a good position to trade out of the pick because it already had Marcus Mariota in place as its franchise QB.

The path to get to No. 2 and select Wentz required some creative work by Roseman. First, he traded 2015 acquisitions Byron Maxwell and Kiko Alonso, along with the No. 13 overall pick, to the Miami Dolphins in exchange for the No. 8 overall pick.

The next step was leapfrogging the Cowboys, who held the No. 4 overall pick. Roseman worked his magic once again.

Philadelphia acquired the No. 2 pick in 2016 and a 2017 fourth-round pick in exchange for the No. 8 pick in 2016, the No. 77 pick (third round) in 2016, the No. 100 pick (fourth round) in 2016, a 2017 first-rounder, and a 2018 second-rounder.

Suddenly the top two picks were guaranteed to be quarterbacks. The question came down to who would go where. The Eagles got all indications that Jared Goff was going to be selected by the Rams. That meant they would end up getting their man in Wentz.

Just like that, Wentz became a sure-fire top-two pick. As expected, Goff went first overall with Philadelphia selecting Wentz soon afterward.

Wentz's wild rise was complete, and the Eagles got their man. ★

Wentz runs a drill at the NFL Combine on Saturday, February 27, 2016, in Indianapolis. (AP Photo/Darron Cummings)

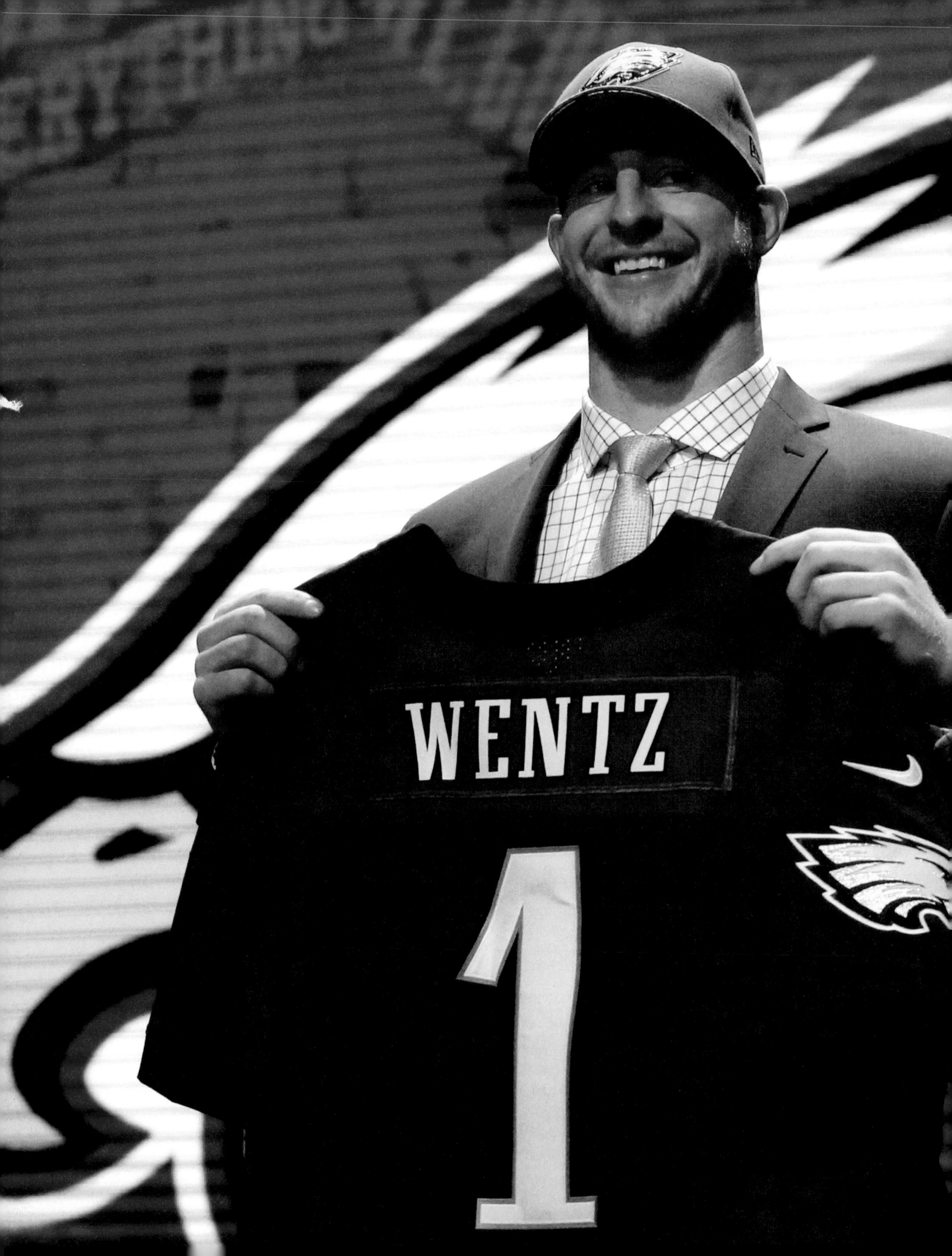
WENTZ
1

Wentz poses for photos after being selected by the Philadelphia Eagles with the second overall pick in the 2016 NFL Draft, Thursday, April 28, 2016, in Chicago. (AP Photo/Charles Rex Arbogast)

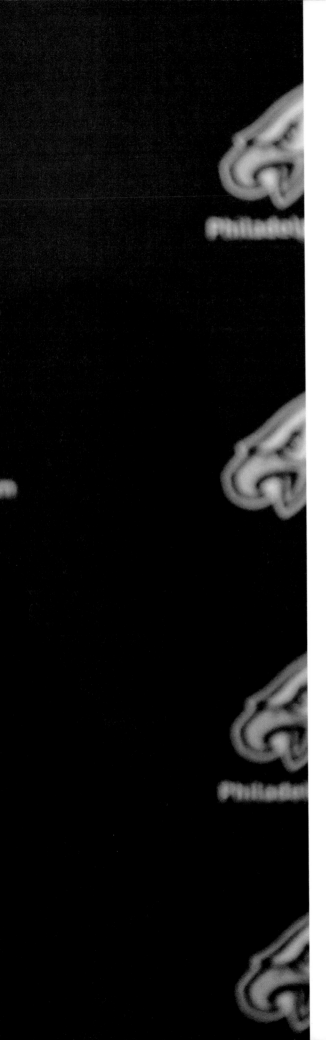

Ready to Fly Like an Eagle

Carson Wentz was eager to go to work as soon as he heard his name called with the Eagles on the clock with the No. 2 overall pick. He pretty much knew that Philadelphia was going to be his new home soon after the team traded up in the draft.

Wentz was entering a locker room as the future cornerstone of the franchise. The Eagles had a nice mix of young and veteran players, but Wentz knew it was the veterans he had to make the biggest impression on.

His approach was to take a blue-collar mentality and show that he was willing to put in the work to eventually lead the organization to big things. For Wentz, it was all about respect.

"You have to earn it, you have to earn that respect," Wentz said during a group interview the day before the draft. "You have to put in the hard work. You've got to have the 'first one in and the last one out' type of mentality. That's how I've always been. Obviously, the

Wentz answers a question during a news conference at the Eagles' practice facility, Friday, April 29, 2016, in Philadelphia. (AP Photo/Rich Schultz)

best way to earn that respect is to do well. Go out and compete, succeed, and I'm looking forward to doing that."

Wentz was very engaging with the Philadelphia media, a group known for its aggressive coverage of the Eagles. While on his first conference call, Wentz told the reporters that he heard they are tough and couldn't wait to meet them.

It was like he welcomed the challenge of handling one of the largest groups of beat reporters in the NFL. That's Carson Wentz, though. He has a quiet confidence in him and a way of endearing himself to people that he encounters.

From the outside looking in, things weren't ideal for Wentz when he was first drafted. The Eagles had just re-signed quarterback Sam Bradford, and Doug Pederson brought former Chiefs quarterback Chase Daniel with him from Kansas City with the promise that he would be able to compete for a starting spot.

Bradford stormed out of the Eagles facility when he first heard news of the trade. He refused to return for voluntary organized activities and demanded a trade.

Executive VP Howie Roseman knew the situation wasn't ideal, but he was confident that Wentz would weather the early storm. Pederson echoed that sentiment when he was asked about the suddenly crowded quarterback room.

"Not at all. When you get a chance to meet Carson, you'll see that he's going to do everything you ask him to do. He's going

to fit perfectly in that room," Pederson said during a press conference after Wentz was drafted. "There's going to be some competition in there, which is great, which I've said all along, and just welcome him to the Eagles."

Wentz had the same mindset when it came to working with Bradford and Daniel. The draft capital that Roseman and the Eagles dealt away in the trade up to get Wentz made it clear that he was the future. In essence, Bradford was a dead man walking as Philadelphia's quarterback.

The dynamic was not the best, but Wentz pledged to make it work.

"The relationship with Sam and the other quarterbacks in the room will be great. It will be a competitive atmosphere," Wentz said during his introductory press conference. "We will all learn together, grow together, and push each other. Ultimately this will lead to benefiting the team and winning a lot of ballgames."

Having spent time waiting his turn at North Dakota State, Wentz understood the idea of developing as a player. Of course, the best way to improve as a football player is to play football, but Wentz was only interested in helping the team become a winner regardless of whether he was under center or helping prepare for game day.

"I learned patience and how to put the team first. I was doing everything I could to help the team, the other quarterback, and grow myself as well," Wentz said. "All I care about is winning. If the team is winning, I

Wentz, second from left, poses with his jersey along with vice president of football operations Howie Roseman, owner Jeffrey Lurie, and head coach Doug Pedreson before a news conference at the team's training facility, Friday, April 29, 2016, in Philadelphia. (AP Photo/Rich Schultz)

Wentz in action with quarterback Sam Bradford (7) during minicamp at the NovaCare Complex, June 7, 2016, in Philadelphia, Pennsylvania. (Cal Sport Media via AP Images/Christopher Szagola/CSM)

"All I care about is winning. If the team is winning, I will do whatever I can to help this team win. It doesn't matter from third-stringer on up, I will do what I have to do to help this team win."

will do whatever I can to help this team win. It doesn't matter from third-stringer on up, I will do what I have to do to help this team win."

Bradford was impressed with Wentz after they spent time together. Wentz's work ethic and willingness to learn was encouraging to Bradford in what seemed like an awkward situation.

"I think he probably went above and beyond what the normal standards would be," Bradford said during a press conference. "You could tell early on that he wants to be great, he works at it, he cares about it, he put in a lot of extra time, and I think it showed up on the field for him. You could see it on the practice field. It seemed like he was always getting better each day that he went out there."

The Eagles made it clear that Wentz was not going to be the starting quarterback. They committed to Bradford and designated Daniel as the backup.

Wentz knew Pederson and the coaching staff were taking a big-picture approach, but he wanted to compete. There was no way he was going to just roll over and accept being

the No. 3 quarterback. He wanted to make it hard for the Eagles to deny him.

"As a competitor, you want to be out there, but I understand that there's a lot to that, and I'm going to just come in and learn and compete. For one, that's not for me to decide," Wentz said. "If I'm not the best at something, it kind of ticks me off and I want to work my tail off to be the best."

The hard work that Wentz put in impressed his teammates. Wentz attacked rookie minicamp and took command of the huddle. It was clear that he was the leader of the rookies.

Wentz delighted the media members who were there to cover his first time wearing an Eagles uniform. Heading into rookie minicamp, his vertical passing ability was something that he wanted to improve upon.

That's exactly what Wentz did as he connected with some of his rookie teammates for deep passes. A few of those throws came at the expense of North Dakota State teammate and cornerback C.J. Smith.

Wentz got his first interaction with the whole team when it was time to report to minicamp with the veterans. They respected his command of the huddle and how well

Wentz made his debut in the first preseason game against the Tampa Bay Buccaneers.

he was able to recite the lengthy West Coast offense play calls.

Even though Wentz was named the No. 3 quarterback, the ball had a different zip when it came out of his hands. Granted, the issues that he had as far as connecting on deep crossing and dig routes resurfaced.

Once training camp rolled around, Wentz remained the No. 3 quarterback, but the reps were evenly distributed. Wentz continued to impress with his big arm while Bradford displayed his surgical accuracy.

The two quarterbacks have different styles but seemed to be caught in a game of "anything you can do, I can do better." Pederson liked the aggressive nature that Wentz brought when he was on the field.

"He has a natural ability to throw the ball down the field, and that's what you like," Pederson said. "You love the aggression. You want to be able to push it down the field. And some of it is by play design and some of it is just by sheer mistake. But man, I love seeing the ball go over the top at times."

Wentz made his debut in the first preseason game against the Tampa Bay Buccaneers. He came in on the final drive of the second quarter and didn't leave until late in the fourth.

The crowd went wild when his name was announced as he trotted onto the field. Pederson told him to give a thumbs up to make sure Wentz heard his voice as the head coach spoke to him via the microphone in his helmet.

Wentz obliged and gave the thumbs up before huddling up. The fans at Lincoln Financial Field thought the thumbs up was to them and went wild. The relationship between Wentz and the fans was sealed at that moment.

Wentz showed the same disregard for his body as he did at North Dakota State. Unfortunately, Wentz suffered a cracked rib when he took a big hit during the game. He was on the shelf for the rest of the preseason.

The Eagles held an open practice at Lincoln Financial Field for the fans the following week. No Eagles player got more cheers than Wentz did, and all he did was walk out of the tunnel in shorts, a hat, and his jersey!

It was going to be hard for the fans to accept Wentz not being on the field at some point in the 2016 season. Fortunately for all parties involved, they didn't have to. ★

Wentz takes a hit from Buccaneers linebacker Micah Awe (44) after getting the pass off during the second half of a preseason game against Tampa Bay , Thursday, August 11, 2016, in Philadelphia. The Eagles won 17-9. (AP Photo/Chris Szagola)

Wentz in action during the first half against the Cleveland Browns, Sunday, September 11, 2016, in Philadelphia. (AP Photo/Matt Rourke)

The QB Incubator

The Eagles set up an environment to support the development of Carson Wentz. They have two former NFL quarterbacks on the staff in head coach Doug Pederson and offensive coordinator Frank Reich. Quarterbacks coach John DeFilippo played the position in college.

Just for good measure, backup quarterback Chase Daniel was in place to help Wentz learn the offense and add a set of experienced eyes to support him from the sideline. Wentz saw right away how he could learn from the veteran quarterbacks already on the roster.

"When I first got here, it was good to have Sam and Chase and the coaches," Wentz said during the start of minicamp, "But I really talked with Sam quite a bit and Chase and just really wanted to dive deeper into this offense.

"Sam had some good insight on our offense and also he was in a number of (other) systems as well, so they were really good conversations and really built a good relationship with him and I'm looking forward to playing with them."

Entering training camp, Pederson had no intentions of playing Wentz early in the season. In fact, Wentz was not even supposed to suit up on game day.

The idea of having a player that a team traded up to select at No. 2 not active on game days was mind-boggling. Yet that was Pederson's plan.

The decision didn't seem to be one that offensive coordinator Frank Reich was on the same page with. He opened up about wanting to see an actual competition to determine the starter, rather than have the job given to incumbent quarterback Sam Bradford.

In all honesty, Reich was right. Bradford, Daniel, and Wentz should have all been given a chance to win the job.

With Bradford's extensive injury history, it was likely that he would go down at some point during the season. If Bradford went down, Chase Daniel would have been given a chance to take over.

Wentz goes over plays with quarterback Daniel Chase during a game against the Cleveland Browns at Lincoln Financial Field in Philadelphia, Sunday, September 11, 2016. (Winslow Townson/AP Images for Panini)

Meanwhile, Wentz continued to spend extra time in the film room studying with all of the pieces in place to ease his transition. Like Pederson, Daniel served as a backup to some pretty good quarterbacks, including Drew Brees and Alex Smith.

Pederson always appreciated how Daniel helped Smith prepare for game day. He expected to see the same thing happen in Philadelphia. With Daniel having spent three seasons with Pederson in Kansas City, he was well-versed in the offense that was brought to the Eagles.

Knowing the terminology like the back of his hand, it was easy for Daniel to help the other quarterbacks understand the scheme. It also helped that Philadelphia used a lot of concepts similar to the one Wentz ran in college.

Wentz is familiar with the West Coast system. He learned the offense while he was at North Dakota State. Wentz had the freedom to change pass protection, change the play call, and run read-pass options.

Even though he went to a smaller school, Wentz was more prepared than other players such as Jared Goff who played in air-raid offenses and looked at a card with a picture on it to get the play call.

The Eagles staff honed in on Wentz's familiarity with the West Coast concepts by giving him more reps in minicamp and training camp. Wentz began to get more comfortable with the playbook, which helped him play fast.

Wentz listens to head coach Doug Pederson during rookie minicamp at the NovaCare Complex in Philadelphia. (Christopher Szagola/CSM via AP Images)

Another part of Wentz's development in the QB Incubator was his mechanics. With so much going on and so much information to process, a lot of times a quarterback falls victim to being swallowed by the moment.

"Just trying to make sure his lower half of his body is in a better posture. Specifically trying to keep his feet tighter to the ground," Pederson said during training camp. "He can get a little jumpy, a little hoppy. He can also be a little upright in his frame, so try to keep him in a bent posture a little bit. Sometimes he can get a little tall, and sometimes that affects your throw."

The mechanics became an on-going issue that would be tweaked over the 2016 season, leading to Wentz going and working with a QB coach before the start of his second season.

DeFilippo worked extensively with Wentz during practice to improve his footwork in the pocket and help him focus on keeping his eyes down the field.

The focus on seeing the field while moving within the pocket didn't pay off as much initially, but it definitely showed when Wentz took the field for the 2017 season opener against the Washington Redskins.

The Eagles' first touchdown of the season came when Wentz managed to escape pressure in the pocket and ran to his left side only to see wide receiver Nelson Agholor turn up the field. Wentz reset his feet just like he and DeFilippo worked on before unleashing a beautiful deep pass to

Wentz heads out to the practice field during training camp, Tuesday, July 26, 2016, in Philadelphia. (AP Photo/Chris Szagola)

Agholor, who caught the ball and ran to the end zone for a 58-yard touchdown.

Creating big plays through the quarterback scramble drill when things break down became a staple of the Eagles offense. Wentz suddenly became a quarterback who was known just as much for the ability to freelance as he was for his pocket passing ability.

Wentz's improvement from his rookie season to a second-year quarterback was an integral part of Philadelphia's success. The Eagles staff honed in on taking Wentz's game to the next level.

They implemented more situational periods of practice to focus on making Wentz and the offense more efficient on third down. The focus on working through reads quickly and going where the scheme took him allowed Wentz to spread the ball around more and created opportunities for all of the pass catchers to be involved.

Philadelphia's offense became much more efficient on third downs because of the focus on improving in that area. Wentz delivered in 3rd-and-long situations for some of the most significant plays of the season.

Pederson and the staff helped Wentz elevate his game from promising rookie to lead one of the league's most balanced attacks. The arrow was definitely pointing up for Wentz. ★

Philadelphia Eagles head coach Doug Pederson talks to Wentz during practice at training camp, Monday, July 25, 2016, in Philadelphia. (AP Photo/Chris Szagola)

Wentz throws a pass as offensive guard Allen Barbre (76) tries to block Pittsburgh Steelers defensive end Cameron Heyward (97), Sunday, September 25, 2016, in Philadelphia. The Eagles won 34-3. (AP Photo/Chris Szagola)

Thrown Into the Fire

September 3, 2016, will be a day that Carson Wentz remembers for the rest of his life. One week before the season opener, the Eagles traded starting quarterback Sam Bradford to the Minnesota Vikings for a first-round pick.

Executive VP Howie Roseman caught the Vikings in a desperate situation after their starting quarterback, Teddy Bridgewater, went down with a severe knee injury. The Vikings felt they had a championship caliber team entering the season and offensive coordinator Pat Shurmur had previous experience with Bradford.

Getting Ready for Cleveland

The trade cleared the way for Wentz to be the starter despite initial expectations to be the No. 3 quarterback and not even suit up on game day. Wentz was suddenly the starter in the season opener against the Cleveland Browns despite limited reps in the preseason.

The rib injury that Wentz sustained in the preseason opener against the Buccaneers still lingered, but it was not going to stop him from being ready. Head coach Doug Pederson said Wentz was healthy and did everything with the first-team offense during practice.

Wentz practiced with extra protection on his ribs to give him a feel for what he'd have on for game day. Pederson looked forward

Wentz passes for his first career touchdown during the first half against the Cleveland Browns, Sunday, September 11, 2016, in Philadelphia. (AP Photo/Matt Rourke)

to the season opener with anticipation as Wentz was set to make his first career start.

"I'm excited. I'm thrilled that this is an opportunity for him," Pederson said during a press conference before the game. "It's an opportunity for our organization, our team. We're going full steam ahead. So I feel fully confident that we'll go get the job done."

Bradford was a favorite in the locker room. He earned respect from the other veteran players because of the way he handled the Wentz situation after initially walking away.

The veteran quarterback was razor-sharp in practice and impressed in the preseason. The team had division championship aspirations with Bradford under center. Would those expectations remain in place with Bradford gone?

Pederson was able to get a gauge for how the locker room felt after they saw Bradford get traded.

"Guys are excited. Guys are excited about Carson," Pederson said. "Obviously, when you lose your quarterback in Sam, it can be mixed emotions. But the guys were 100 percent behind it and thrilled that Carson is going to be the guy. They've seen him day in and day out like we've seen him. They know he can be a special player in this league. They've embraced it and are supporting him 100 percent."

The mindset that comes with being the quarterback is unique. It's hard to prepare for the pressure that is placed on

Philadelphia Eagle Ryan Mathews (24) and Wentz celebrate after Matthews' touchdown during the second half against the Cleveland Browns, Sunday, September 11, 2016, in Philadelphia. (AP Photo/Michael Perez)

Wentz cracks a smile during a break against the Cleveland Browns. (Winslow Townson/AP Images for Panini)

The mindset that comes with being the quarterback is unique. It's hard to prepare for the pressure that is placed on the quarterback, especially in such a quick turnaround.

the quarterback, especially in such a quick turnaround.

Pederson was confident in Wentz's ability to handle the new responsibility. That made the decision to start him an easy one.

"He's such a special guy that this doesn't bother him. The stage is not that big. He can handle this. That's why making this decision is very comforting to me and really easy to make," said Pederson. "Just knowing him and knowing how he prepares, and knowing what he's done in the past. This guy is a proven winner. He's proved it all the way up through college, and we fully expect him to do the same thing at this level. He's such a smart guy. I keep saying this, but I see it day in and day out. Carson is a sharp learner. He makes a mistake once, he can move on from it."

Pederson and the coaching staff went back to the Bucs game to see some of the things that worked well for Wentz. They also incorporated some of the things Wentz did at North Dakota State to make him more comfortable with the sudden transition from backup to starter.

Wentz had shown that he is comfortable on the move. The Eagles implemented several bootleg plays that let him roll out

and make an easy read while scanning a condensed portion of the field.

A lot of the throws that he was asked to make were quick reads. The offense was designed to make the decision-making more comfortable for him.

Finding a Safety Blanket

Wentz delivered his first touchdown pass as a pro to wide receiver Jordan Matthews. He had perfect placement on the throw that dropped just over the receiver's shoulder in the end zone for the score.

Matthews would become one of Wentz's favorite targets during his rookie season. Their first game set the tone. Wentz connected with Matthews seven times for 114 yards and a touchdown.

Having Matthews was a safety blanket for Wentz because of the familiarity they had after spending time together during training camp. Like Wentz, Matthews suffered an injury that kept him out of the lineup for some time.

They spent time together in the training room and on the field as Matthews ran routes to test his injured ankle. Wentz threw him passes as he worked his way back from the rib injury. The chemistry was formed there.

Coming Out with a Bang

Philadelphia jumped out to a 3–0 record in Wentz's first three games, which included a 300-yard passing performance against the Pittsburgh Steelers in Week 3. Wentz was named the Pepsi Rookie of the Week after each of the first two games in 2016.

His standout performance against the Steelers earned him NFC Offensive Player of the Week honors.

As a rookie, Wentz started all 16 games for the Eagles as they finished the season with a 7–9 record. He completed a league-rookie-record 379 passes as a rookie, breaking the record of 354, held by none other than Sam Bradford, when he was with the St. Louis Rams in 2010.

The 379 completions is also a single-season franchise record, breaking another record held by Bradford, when he completed 346 passes in 2015. Wentz also set a single-season franchise record with 607 pass attempts, which was the second-highest number of attempts by a rookie in league history. Andrew Luck holds the record with 627 completions as a rookie with the Indianapolis Colts, in 2012.

After a rough stretch in which the Eagles lost five consecutive games, the season ended on an upswing with two wins in a row for Philadelphia. Wentz was thrown into the fire but weathered the storm and came out on top. ★

Wentz scrambles against the Dallas Cowboys, Sunday, January 1, 2017, in Philadelphia. The Eagles won 27-13. (Al Tielemans via AP Images)

Wentz scrambles away from New York Giant Romeo Okwara (78) during the second half, Thursday, December 22, 2016, in Philadelphia. (AP Photo/Michael Perez)

Faith and Football

Carson Wentz is heavily invested in his relationship with God. Growing up, Wentz's life was consumed by sports, but he went to a Lutheran church and was confirmed. Wentz said he thought he was right with God because he was a good kid and went to church.

His faith has expanded to a foundation that he calls AO1, short for Audience of One. The foundation was launched in 2017. Its mission is to "demonstrate the love of God by providing opportunities and support for the less fortunate and those in need."

On his foundation's website, Wentz opened up about how his faith grew while he was at North Dakota State University. College is a time when people can form some of their less memorable relationships. For Wentz, it was a time when he developed the best.

"My head was spinning. I had just learned new language in install meetings and Dante (senior quarterback Dante Perez) says, 'Hey, ever read the Bible?' I'm like, 'We're at football practice, not right now.' Then we started talking, ended up meeting, and he kind of mentored me in my faith for about a year. Dante was huge, I owe him a lot."

Wentz met with Perez once a week throughout the year and read the New Testament. He quickly developed a thirst to learn more about God and became an active member of the team Bible study, as well as regularly attending church. Through football, Wentz was exposed to God and cultivated a great relationship that still leads his life today. He even had AO1 tattooed on the bottom of his right wrist.

"It was kind of a motto I picked up early in my career, and I finally put it on my body just to live with Jesus as my audience. Whether it is playing football, going to school, or whatever I'm doing, I'm doing it for the Lord as my audience," said Wentz on his foundation's website.

Sharing the Word

Wentz delivered a sermon during the summer of 2017 at First Assembly Church in Fargo, North Dakota. He opened up about his faith in the sermon and discussed a recent mission that opened his eyes.

Wentz's cleat during practice at the team's NFL football training facility in Philadelphia. (AP Photo/Matt Rourke)

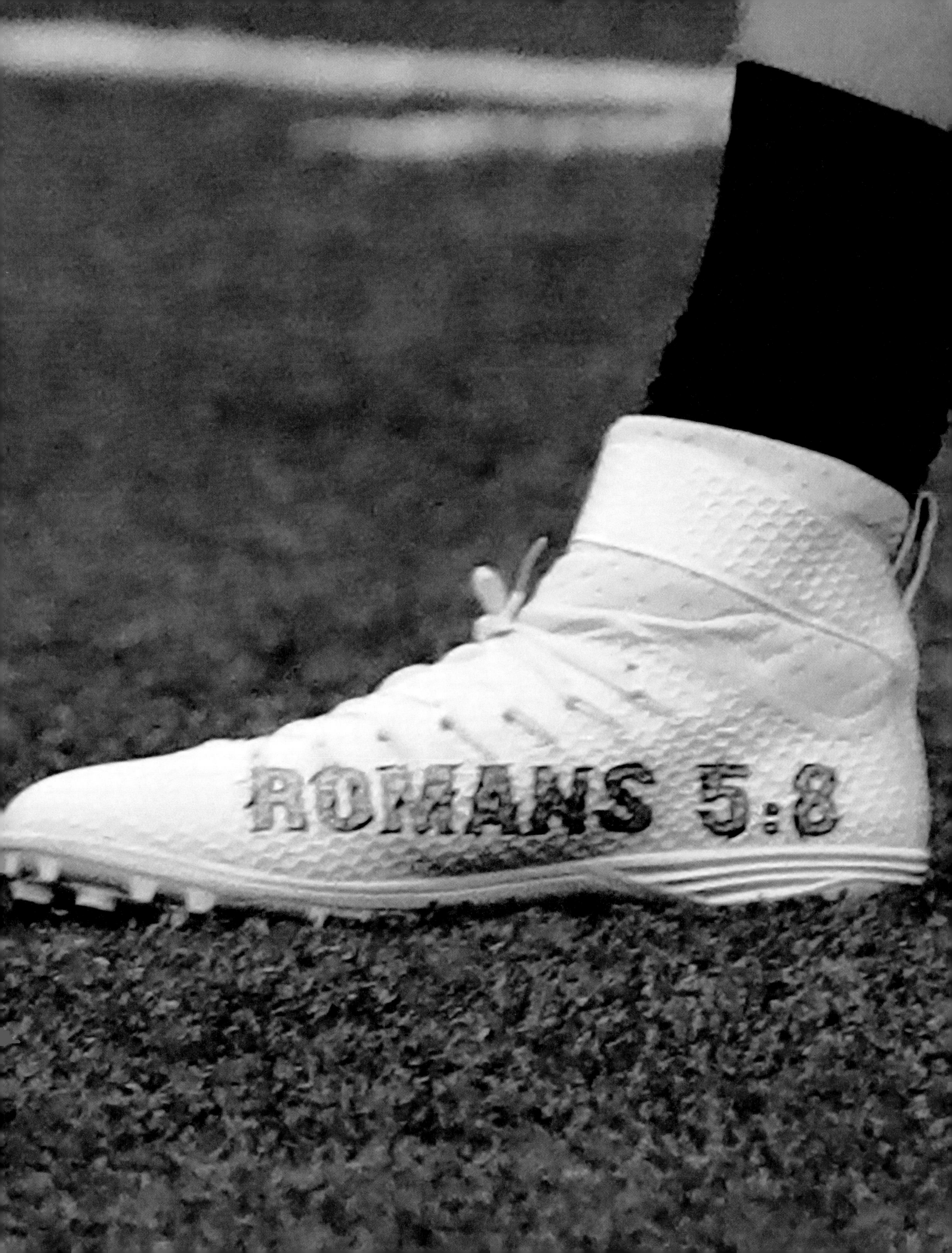
ROMANS 5:8

"I want to take all the attention off of myself, and give it to God," Wentz said to open his sermon before pointing to John 5:19: "Very truly I tell you, the Son can do nothing by himself; he can do only what he sees his Father doing, because whatever the Father does the Son also does."

Wentz explained how walking step by step with The Father is what allowed him to know to do the good work. He went on to share his experience on a mission in Haiti with former Eagles teammate Jordan Matthews.

Wentz, Matthews, and a group of church members went to Port-au-Prince, Haiti. His AO1 Foundation provided funds to Mission of Hope to help build a multipurpose sports complex and education center on campus.

"I believe in Mission of Hope's initiative completely," Wentz said in a statement. "I feel that this sports complex will be an incredible way for the youth of Haiti to have more opportunities to enjoy sporting competition, to further their education, to have access to healthy meals, and to enjoy being around a Christian community to help further their faith."

While there, they preached to the people in the village. Wentz helped kids paint their own houses. He said the kids tried to take the paint brush out of his hands to help with the painting. Wentz even lifted some of the kids up to allow them to paint higher spots on the walls. Considering he is 6-foot-5, those kids probably got to see things from a brand-new perspective!

The trip forced Wentz to take a new approach to things.

Wentz bows in prayer with Eagles and Vikings after their game, Sunday, October 23, 2016, in Philadelphia. The Eagles won 21-10. (AP Photo/Chris Szagola)

"I just went to a whole new country, needed an interpreter," Wentz said. "I walked up to these people in these villages, talked to them and gave them the gospel, and I can barely turn to my neighbor back home?"

He came back with a new mission, which was to take advantage of every opportunity to share the gospel. Wentz felt challenged to a daily mission.

In Wentz's case, he never tries to force his faith on anyone. His mission is to just plant the seed.

It was only fitting that Wentz concluded his sermon in North Dakota State by saying, "If you were standing before God tonight, and He asks you what you've done to enter into His kingdom, what would you say?"

Then he invited anyone who wanted to find a closer relationship with Jesus to raise their hand. "Don't be shy, Jesus wants to call you home," Wentz said before he closed with a prayer.

Landing in the Right Place

Before the 2016 NFL Draft, Wentz prayed and asked that he would land in a place where he can grow his faith. Ending up with the Eagles was a blessing.

The team holds weekly Bible study at the facility as well as couples night at various player's houses. Many of the players have a close relationship with the team's pastor, Theodore Winsley.

Pastor Ted has been serving the players for 16 years. It all started with Troy Vincent for Pastor Ted. Vincent wanted the word to

Wentz warms up before a game against the Denver Broncos, Sunday, November 5, 2017, in Philadelphia. (AP Photo/Michael Perez)

Having the quarterback is the key to creating a strong culture of faith for the team.

be taught and gave the ministry access to the player's lives.

There is a rich tradition of faith among the Eagles that goes back to defensive end Reggie White, who passed it on to Vincent, then to safety Brian Dawkins, then wide receiver Jason Avant and quarterback Nick Foles, and ultimately to Wentz.

Pastor Ted says this group is like a committee which consists of Carson, safety Chris Maragos, tight end Zach Ertz, tight end Trey Burton, and linebacker Jordan Hicks, among others.

Having the quarterback is the key to creating a strong culture of faith for the team, according to Pastor Ted.

"Once you get the quarterback, you have the team. When Nick Foles came as the starting quarterback and a strong believer, the culture was solidified," said Pastor Ted.

Foles is the reason the Eagles have Bible study at the facility on Thursday nights. He is also the reason why the Bible study starts even before the regular season.

Now with Wentz in place, the ministry can continue to be strong. Players such as linebacker Mychal Kendricks and wide receiver Marcus Johnson have even gotten baptized.

Pastor Ted said he saw something in Wentz from the first time he sat next to him at a team rookie symposium at the Novacare complex.

"From the very first moment he came to the team, he made it evident that he was a believer. Carson came to the Bible study, and his quiet boldness, his presence, his genuineness...He has a strong sense of who he is," Pastor Ted said. "He is not loud, and he is not boisterous. When he speaks, you hear him. It's deliberate, and he doesn't need a lot of words. It showed immediately in Bible study. He's respectful, but he is still a leader. He takes charge only when he believes he is supposed to."

Pastor Ted helps players understand that football is not their purpose—it's their platform. Faith has a way of grounding players.

"Football is a very short part of their lives," Pastor Ted explained. "If they don't understand that, they get caught up. In Philadelphia, football is looked at as a god. Without this grounding, they get crushed by it instead of standing on the platform of it."

The way Wentz has handled all of the early success with ease can be attributed to his faith. It allows Wentz to put things in proper perspective.

"At the end of the day, he loves the game but has a really good understanding that it is just a game," said Pastor Ted.

It is easy to see why the Eagles locker room is so well rooted in its faith. ★

Carson Wentz, "The Hunter"

Like most people, Carson Wentz has ways to unwind and get his mind off of things. Wentz was exposed to hunting when he was a kid. His fondness for it grew once he got to college, especially when he got a chance to get out with some of his friends.

"I really fell in love with it when I was in college. It was a kind of new experience with a couple of buddies," Wentz said. "I got into bow hunting later in college and was like, this is so peaceful. You sit in the woods. The majority of the hunting that I do is super relaxing. In the off-season, I do stuff in the mountains."

Wentz saves the more adventurous hunting trips for when he isn't playing football, during the off-season. During the season Wentz enjoys simply sitting in a tree relaxing for a couple of hours. He wears a harness just in case he gets too relaxed and falls asleep.

Wentz loves hunting so much he bought guns for the offensive linemen as Christmas presents. He took them hunting in May of 2017.

The downtime in between targets is relaxing for Wentz, but when what he's looking for comes his way, he flips the switch.

"For me, it's just the most relaxing thing," Wentz said. "But when there are animals— whether it's deer hunting or bird hunting—it gives you that adrenaline rush. It's that adrenaline rush that gets you fired up."

Of all places to be, Wentz was laying in the middle of a cornfield when he found out about the Sam Bradford trade that would change his rookie season. Wentz said he was able to get one goose before the news but plans changed once he was told.

His weapon of choice during the season is a crossbow. Wentz said he just sits there most of the time not shooting at anything. There may be deer here and there, but the big catch is when a buck wanders through.

"You wait for that one big buck and it's just like, when it happens, that adrenaline rush is unbelievable," Wentz explained as his tone changed. "When it doesn't happen, you are just thankful. You appreciate nature. It's a chance to just decompress. It gets my mind right and it's just like the most relaxing, peaceful thing that anyone can do."

Some people like to ride bikes or go hiking to escape the daily grind. Wentz likes to hunt. It also allows him to spend time with his brother.

"My brother and I hunt together all the time," Wentz said. "One of us is usually filming. We hunt together and it's a way for us to bond as well."

They've chronicled their hunting adventures back home in North Dakota and as far away as New Zealand. ■

Wentz kneels in prayer with teammates following practice at training camp, Tuesday, July 26, 2016, in Philadelphia. (AP Photo/Chris Szagola)

A Leader of Men

Carson Wentz became the leader of the Eagles in the locker room and on the field soon after he took over as the starting quarterback. His focus on hard work and command of the huddle resonated with the team as soon as he got to the NovaCare Complex.

As a rookie starting quarterback, Wentz had to be able to look at the other 10 guys in the huddle and convince them they can win against any circumstances. That's a hard job to ask a younger player to carry out, but it's a task that Wentz does naturally.

"I thought that was all kind of natural, things naturally happened," Wentz said. "Yes, I was a rookie, but I don't think that I was by any means quiet. I wasn't just the guy that rolled with the punches and went with it. I thought I was still doing my job as a leader as well. But the longer we're playing this game and the more experience we have, the more we can just step up our leadership as well."

Wentz breathed life into the Eagles starting with his performance against the Cleveland Browns in the

Wentz and Zach Ertz walk off the field after the Eagles beat the Cleveland Browns, Sunday, September 11, 2016, in Philadelphia. (AP Photo/Michael Perez)

season opener. Other players naturally follow his lead.

"He's going to be in the film room as much as anyone on the team. I think you love that at the quarterback position, that he's going to the most prepared guy on the team," tight end Zach Ertz said.

Eagles safety Malcolm Jenkins is one of the team captains. He admired how Wentz quickly earned the team's confidence.

"From a veteran on the team, I think everyone has a lot of confidence in Carson," Jenkins said last season. "You know that even if he makes mistakes, he's not going to be gun-shy, and he's not going to let the mistake ruin his day."

Wentz's leadership extended to the off-season when he made arrangements for the receivers and Ertz to spend a week with him at home in North Dakota.

Newly signed teammate Alshon Jeffery was the first player to arrive in Fargo, North Dakota, for Wentz's passing camp. Jeffery signed with Philadelphia because he wanted Wentz to be his quarterback.

The trip to North Dakota was an opportunity for Wentz and the receivers to further develop chemistry. Wentz gave them a taste of the North Dakota lifestyle by introducing them to Bison burgers.

They ran routes and worked on timing with Wentz on an outdoor field at North Dakota State University. The gathering set the tone for when the players reported to training camp later that month.

Once training camp rolled around, it was all hands on deck. Wentz was the first one on the field and ready to go to work.

He started getting every receiver involved right away and pushed them to compete. Wentz was always the first to arrive at the different stations to begin various portions of practice.

Before Jordan Matthews was traded during training camp, he noticed a slight difference in Wentz as he entered his second season. There was no question the Eagles were his team.

"There's definitely a poise about him. You can tell it's not like last year, when he was thrust into the position," Matthews said. "He knows his role, he knows he's the guy, and I think there's a sense of confidence that comes with that, a sense of poise that he handles extremely well. I'm excited to see what he does this whole off-season and what we're going to do moving forward."

Wentz sprinted from place to place on the field. It was Wentz who broke the offense down before heading into team periods of practice. It's those kinds of little things that help reinforce Wentz's presence as a leader.

Head coach Doug Pederson likes the command of the huddle that he sees from Wentz. There is a lot more communication before and after reps in practice.

"He steps in there with a lot of confidence, and that's what you want. He's leading the football team," Pederson said proudly when asked about Wentz during training camp.

Philadelphia Eagles wide receiver Alshon Jeffery (17) talks with Wentz during a preseason game against the Miami Dolphins on Thursday, August 24, 2017, in Philadelphia. (Aaron M. Sprecher via AP)

Wide receiver Torrey Smith came to the Eagles during the off-season. Like the other wideouts, he spent time with Wentz in North Dakota. Soon after meeting Wentz he started to notice the intangible qualities that make the quarterback a leader.

"It didn't take long to see that he's got it. He's a guy you want to play for and play with," Smith said before the season started. "I look at him in the huddle and, man, I can't wait to see what it's going to be like on game day. He's not going to be flustered. He's going out there making great throws, so we know that if we do our jobs, we're going to make big plays."

"I am wired that way. I like to be the guy in charge. I like to have the ball in my hand," Wentz told 94WIP during the bye week. "A good leader is someone who can make everyone around him better. I heard the term 'servant leader,' which is kind of like always being willing to do anything for my guys. That's what it comes down to for me. I want to make everyone around me better."

When the Eagles are on the road, Wentz leads them onto the field as they are announced as the visiting team. Wentz runs out waving his arms, challenging the crowd to make noise.

If the Eagles are going to get to the Super Bowl, it will be Wentz who leads the way. ★

Philadelphia Eagles receiver Torrey Smith and Wentz celebrate after Smith's touchdown during the first half of a preseason game against the Miami Dolphins, Thursday, August 24, 2017, in Philadelphia. (AP Photo/Michael Perez)

Philadelphia Eagle Zach Ertz (86) celebrates his touchdown catch from Wentz during the first half, Sunday, January 1, 2017, in Philadelphia. (AP Photo/Michael Perez)

Wentz vs. Prescott

Having been selected in the same draft by two divisional rivals, Dallas Cowboys quarterback Dak Prescott and Carson Wentz will always be tied together. The two even faced each other in the Senior Bowl before the draft.

Wentz started the game and only played in the first quarter for the North team that was led by Dallas head coach Jason Garrett and his staff. He completed 6-of-10 passes for 50 yards. Two of Wentz's incompletions came as a result of dropped passes.

Prescott came away with the game MVP honors after completing 7-of-10 passes for 61 yards and a touchdown.

Now they will do battle for years to come with Prescott's Cowboys going against Wentz's Eagles. Although the Cowboys and Eagles played each other twice during the 2016–17 season, Prescott only played in one of the games. Dallas squeaked out a close win over the Eagles at home in Week 8, when Prescott delivered a game-winning five-yard touchdown pass to tight end Jason Witten in overtime to secure the win.

Wentz held his own in a losing effort against Dallas by completing 32-of-43 pass attempts for 202 yards and a touchdown. Prescott countered with 287 yards on 39 pass attempts to go along with two touchdowns and an interception.

Prescott and the Cowboys got off to a hot start in 2016. They finished the season with a 13–3 record to capture the NFC East division title.

Dallas had the division title wrapped up by the time the two teams faced each other in the regular season finale.

As a rookie, Prescott threw for 3,667 yards and 23 touchdowns with just four interceptions. Both quarterbacks took turns setting the NFL record for consecutive passes without an interception by a rookie.

Dallas Cowboys quarterback Dak Prescott (4) greets Wentz after the Cowboys played the Eagles, Sunday, October 30, 2016, in Arlington, Texas. (Greg Trott via AP)

Prescott ended up with the record, after his 178th throw was picked off by Green Bay Packers safety Morgan Burnett. As rookies, Prescott had the edge over Wentz after winning Offensive Rookie of the Year honors.

Some dismissed Prescott's season because he had a strong supporting cast. Having good players helps, but make no mistake about it— Prescott had the most prominent role in his success as a rookie.

The Eagles followed the Cowboys' lead in 2017. They added Alshon Jeffery and LeGarrette Blount to give Wentz more firepower on game days.

Wentz got off to an incredible start in 2017. He ranked among the league leaders in touchdown passes and has become an ultra-effective quarterback on third downs. The Eagles jumped out to the league's best record, and Wentz was mentioned as an MVP candidate.

Any conversation about Prescott and Wentz is usually fueled by emotion. For some reason, it's not okay to believe both are good quarterbacks. The truth is both are solid quarterbacks who will lead their teams and the NFC East back to being among the league's best.

When Doug Pederson first took over as head coach of the Eagles, he planned to have Sam Bradford as his quarterback and then draft a player who could develop into the starter after Bradford played out the second year of his contract.

Prescott was one of the quarterbacks Philadelphia was interested in before making the trades to get into a position to draft Wentz. The Eagles had Prescott visit with the team at the NovaCare complex. They even put him

Wentz points out the Dallas Cowboys defense, Sunday, October 30, 2016, in Arlington, Texas. (James D. Smith via AP)

Wentz rolls out and eludes a defender during an NFL Thursday Night Football game against the New York Giants, Thursday, December 22, 2016, in Philadelphia. The Eagles won 24–19. (Paul Jasienski via AP)

through a mock press conference to see how he would respond to Philadelphia's tough media.

By some measures, Prescott reminds NFL personnel people of former Eagles quarterback Donovan McNabb. Pederson was in Philadelphia when McNabb was selected with the No. 2 pick in 1999. Pederson's mentor Andy Reid found a great deal of success with McNabb. Perhaps Pederson was looking for his own version when they brought Prescott in for a closer look.

Meanwhile, Wentz and the Cowboys went through an extensive feeling-out process during the Senior Bowl. It seemed like Wentz was going to be the pick for Dallas, who held the No. 4 pick.

Executive VP Howie Roseman pulled off a couple of trades to get to No.2 overall in the 2016 NFL Draft. Those trades set off a role reversal. As a result, the Cowboys took running back Ezekiel Elliott No. 4 overall.

The Eagles drafted what they thought was going to be a developmental prospect while the Cowboys rushed Prescott into action after starter Tony Romo went down with a back injury during the preseason.

It's incredible how the two quarterbacks' careers are intertwined. Like Prescott, Wentz got his first start in the NFL due to an injury—on another team.

Bradford was traded to the Vikings when their starting quarterback, Teddy Bridgewater, went down with an injury. That opened the door for Wentz to start the season opener.

Prescott isn't surprised by the success that Wentz has achieved in the NFL.

"He's doing exactly what I thought he'd be doing in this league," Prescott said. "I figured he'd be a good player. Smart guy, great player, great athlete. He's been doing well."

NFL.com draft analyst Daniel Jeremiah polled five NFL executives to see who they would take as their quarterback if they could choose from Wentz, Prescott, and 2016 No. 1 pick Jared Goff.

Two of the executives chose Prescott, while three went with Wentz. Those who took Prescott mentioned his toughness and leadership as their reason. They also felt Prescott was the better thrower.

The ones who took Wentz liked his "football smarts" in addition to his natural arm strength. Given the early success that both franchises have found with their young quarterbacks, either one would be a good choice.

Jeremiah, a former collegiate quarterback himself, chose Wentz out of the three.

"I would still stick with my pre-draft ranking and select Wentz. I love his blend of arm strength, toughness, and creativity. He's on his way to becoming a special player," said Jeremiah.

Perhaps the most entertaining Wentz vs. Prescott debate is on FS1's show *Undisputed*, which features two hours of debate between hosts Skip Bayless and Hall of Fame tight end Shannon Sharpe.

Bayless is known for his outrageous takes. He is a Dallas Cowboys fan and has no problem letting anyone know. It's a foregone conclusion that he would select Prescott over Wentz.

"The Eagles have peaked early, but my Cowboys will peak when it matters," Bayless said after the Eagles pushed their record to 6–1 in 2017. "I'm sorry, I'm still not sold on Carson Wentz and the Eagles. The best quarterback in the NFC East is still Dak Prescott."

Both quarterbacks have shown poise beyond their years. Bayless has no problem giving Prescott credit for helping turn things around for Dallas. But he refuses to acknowledge that Wentz has done the same job in Philadelphia.

"Under fire, when I watch Carson Wentz, I see a deer in headlights," Bayless said. "I don't see the moxie. I don't see the feel. I don't see the command for playing that position that I always see in Dak Prescott."

Bayless took it a step further, adding that Wentz can't change the culture in Philadelphia like Prescott did in Dallas.

"Dak Prescott takes over games with his body language," Bayless continued. "He changed the whole culture of the Cowboys."

Sharpe had a different opinion when faced with the same question.

"The baddest man in the NFC East right now wears No. 11 for the Eagles," Sharpe said on the show in October. "He's a once in a lifetime player. Carson has a better arm. He has a bigger arm than Dak Prescott. He's more mobile than you think. He can get out of harm's way."

Both quarterbacks have their teams in position to compete with any franchise. Prescott led the Cowboys to the NFC East title and the No. 1 seed in the 2016 playoffs before losing to Aaron Rodgers and the Green Bay Packers in the divisional playoff round.

Wentz seems to have the Eagles headed toward a No. 1 seed and NFC East title in 2017–18.

The Wentz vs. Prescott debate will be one that wages on in the future as the two battle for division supremacy. ★

Wentz evades Dallas Cowboys defensive tackle Maliek Collins (96), Sunday, January 1, 2017, in Philadelphia. The Eagles beat the Cowboys 27-13. (AP Photo/Matt Rourke)

Wentz reacts after scoring a rushing touchdown in the fourth quarter against the Baltimore Ravens, December 18, 2016, in Baltimore. The Ravens won 27–26. (Brian Garfinkel via AP)

A Band of Brothers

The Eagles as a whole are a close-knit unit. However, a select group of Eagles drew even closer to each other because of their spiritual commitments. The group really got close during Carson Wentz's rookie season, and their relationship continued to grow during the off-season.

Veteran wide receiver Jordan Matthews established himself as one of Wentz's favorite receivers to target early in the season. Tight end Zach Ertz emerged as another reliable pass catcher down the stretch last year.

The three formed a strong bond that branched out to another tight end, Trey Burton. The group became inseparable. According to Chaplain Theodore Winsley, Burton even held a couples fellowship Bible study at his house.

They attended church together in addition to many other activities outside of the locker room. Safety Chris Maragos was also a part of the group. Together, they took the lead in weekly Bible study held at the facility.

Things seemed to be going well until a trade shook up the group. They lost a member when Matthews was traded to the Buffalo Bills during training camp.

"The only way I can really relate it is like when you're in elementary school or middle school and your best friend growing up," Burton said. "You're going to the same school and then one day his parents move to a different city, and he's gone. And you're like, 'Okay, what the heck do I do?'"

Ertz and Matthews had been teammates since 2014, when Matthews was selected in the second round of the draft. Ertz was a second-round pick in 2013. The two became close friends soon after meeting and formed the foundation of the band of brothers that were a part of the Eagles that included Wentz.

"If it weren't for the Philadelphia Eagles, a kid from Huntsville, Alabama, and a kid from California would have never met," Ertz explained. "He has a brother for life in me, and he knows that. It was emotional for sure, somber. Our group is extremely close."

Philadelphia Eagles tight end Trey Burton, left, and Wentz celebrate a touchdown against the Denver Broncos, Sunday, November 5, 2017, in Philadelphia. (AP Photo/Michael Perez)

Wentz seemed to be the one who was shaken up the most by the trade. He was losing one of his best friends and a security blanket from his rookie season.

"On the personal side, it's tough," Wentz said. "This is my first time experiencing this with someone that's one of my best friends. Seeing him yesterday, it's tough on him, too. It's kind of out of the blue."

Executive VP Howie Roseman knew the relationship that Matthews and Wentz had was intense. That's why he made sure he personally let Wentz know about the deal before it went public. Wentz had no choice but to put faith in the organization and move forward.

Once the deal was done, the group arranged for a final meal together as teammates. They had dinner together at a restaurant near the team's practice facility. Wentz said he drove Matthews to the airport to get on the plane headed to his new team in Buffalo.

The band of spiritual brothers continued after Matthews was traded. Wide receiver Marcus Johnson was baptized before the Eagles Week 6 game against the Carolina Panthers.

Although Maragos is on injured reserve, he is frequently in the building spending time with his teammates. It's a testament to the bond the players share.

Ertz suffered from hamstring tightness in the days leading up to the Eagles' Week

Philadelphia Eagles defensive back Chris Maragos (42) has a laugh with an official as Wentz looks on prior to the coin toss against the Kansas City Chiefs, Sunday, September 17, 2017, in Kansas City. (G. Newman Lowrance via AP)

9 matchup against the Denver Broncos. Up to that point in the 2017 season, the Broncos defense had been allowing an NFL-best 261 yards per game. Wentz was facing the vaunted Denver pass defense known as the "No Fly Zone" without his favorite target. Ertz was ruled out before the game, which meant Burton was going to get an increase in playing time. Wentz gathered Burton and Ertz for a small group prayer before they went through their pregame warmups.

Burton was the recipient of Wentz's third touchdown pass against the Broncos. The magical season continued as the Eagles blew out Denver 51–23. Philadelphia's record stood at 8–1 and was the best in the NFL.

With Burton set to hit free agency after the season, the group should be facing another shakeup. There will likely be teams lining up to pay Burton to be their featured tight end, as opposed to being the Robin to Ertz's Batman.

Surely the pull of his close group of friends will have some influence on his future decision. It'll be a tough decision for him to make. Who knows? Maybe he'll choose to go to the Buffalo Bills to be reunited with Matthews.

Until then, Ertz, Wentz, Maragos, and Burton will continue to enjoy each other's fellowship and look for it to carry them to new heights in 2017–18. ★

Philadelphia Eagles wide receiver Jordan Matthews (81) and Wentz celebrate a touchdown against the Dallas Cowboys on Sunday, October 30, 2016, in Arlington, Texas. (AP Photo/Ron Jenkins)

Wentz throws a pass from the end zone in the second half against the Dallas Cowboys, Sunday, October 30, 2016, in Arlington, Texas. (AP Photo/Michael Ainsworth)

Dressed to Impress

Carson Wentz is dialed in on many things, but putting together the right outfit hasn't always been one of them. Some of the ensembles that he wore during his first postgame press conferences caused local clothiers to cringe.

Fortunately, teammate Malcolm Jenkins opened his own clothing store and has put Wentz in coordinated outfits that are more fitting for a franchise quarterback.

"Carson is pretty bold for a quarterback. He likes prints, patterns, window panes," Jenkins said.

Wentz was happy to work on some new outfits with his teammate's company, Damari Saville.

Jay Amin is Jenkins' partner and oversees the day-to-day operations of Damari Saville. Amin is responsible for helping clients achieve their fashion goals. He worked with Wentz to set up some new looks.

"I could tell that Carson was really trying to set a standard with his look: keeping it business casual and clean-cut, while maintaining his own sense of style and perspective," Amin said as he reflected on working with Wentz during the off-season. "He is a guy who is not afraid of color and has a keen eye for pattern. The main goal with his wardrobe was to focus on fit, integrating his penchant for color and pattern into a consistent style. We took on a less-is-more attitude, focusing on one standout piece per outfit."

"We did a couple of sportcoats, a couple of suits," Wentz said. "I just basically got refitted. My body has kind of changed. I guess everything wasn't tight enough."

Wentz said he doesn't really like to overthink when it comes to creating an outfit. If he likes it, he will go with it.

Wentz responds to questions during a news conference after the Eagles played the Dallas Cowboys on Sunday, October 30, 2016, in Arlington, Texas. (AP Photo/Michael Ainsworth)

Wentz speaks to the media after the Eagles played the Carolina Panthers in Charlotte, Friday, October 13, 2017. (AP Photo/Mike McCarn)

"I just go with what I'm wearing," Wentz said. "I mix it up this year better because I have more, I guess. Home games, I dress up better now. I mean, I feel good with whatever I am wearing so I just make it happen!"

One detail that Wentz does pay attention to is having a scripture monogrammed on the inside of his suits. The scripture is Colossians 3:23. Wentz says it's kind of like his life verse.

"It goes with AO1, which is obviously like my life motto," Wentz said. "It says, 'Whatever you do, work at it with all your heart, as working for the Lord, not for human masters.'

"That correlates with my AO1 motto, where whatever I am doing, I am working for the Lord. That's just a constant reminder. No matter what I am doing, whether it's playing football, whether I am lifting, it's always to glorify Him. He's my audience and it always gives me extra motivation."

Wentz was able to get the help of Fox Sports' Jay Glazer and JC Penney to help him get suited up for the 2016 NFL Draft. (Eagles fans won't want to hear this, but the suit that Wentz wore on draft day was one that came from the Michael Strahan collection.)

With the 2017 NFL Draft taking place in Philadelphia, Wentz was able to coordinate with JC Penney and future Houston Texans quarterback Deshaun Watson. The two came together to donate suits to young men at the Columbia North YMCA in Philadelphia.

Wentz told the kids how he feels more confident when he wears a suit. Watson told the kids about how important it is to make a good first impression. ★

Wentz talks to reporters in the postgame press conference after the Eagles played the Seattle Seahawks in Seattle, Sunday, November 20, 2016. (AP Photo/Stephen Brashear)

Wentz walks outside before a news conference at the Eagles' training facility, Friday, April 29, 2016, in Philadelphia. (AP Photo/Rich Schultz)

The Dutch Destroyer

A couple of years ago, a youth football player in Wilmington, Delaware, dominated on the field. His name was Lukas Kusters, but they called him The Dutch Destroyer because of the way he imposed his will during games.

"Lukas was one of the biggest eight-year-olds I had ever seen," Lukas' coach Raymond Jackson told ESPN's Tom Rinaldi. "They might have a big guy that's busting through the line, and I'd tell Lukas, 'You have to go over there now.' Next thing you know, that kid is laying on the ground."

Unfortunately, after playing in his league's championship, Lukas was diagnosed with a cancerous tumor in his abdomen and the lining of his stomach.

The news was devastating, but the young man refused to give up. He gave cancer a heck of a fight.

While he fought the disease, Lukas found another source of motivation from his favorite team's quarterback.

He loved the Eagles and wanted to play for them when he grew up. Lukas had the team colors on his walls. Wentz and the potential he brought to the Eagles was something that Lukas pulled motivation from.

It was a small thing in comparison to what Lukas was going through, but the future finally looked bright for the Eagles. At the same time, the future suddenly looked bright for young Lukas.

In March of 2017, Lukas returned home after what seemed to be a victory. Lukas and his family celebrated the news that his body was free of cancer.

Unfortunately, the celebration was short-lived. Cancer resurfaced the following month, and this time the doctors told the Kusters family it was unlikely that Lukas would survive.

Wentz greets the family of Lukas Kusters, a young boy who lost his battle with cancer, after the Eagles played the Washington Redskins, Monday, October 23, 2017, in Philadelphia. The Eagles won 34-24. (AP Photo/Matt Rourke)

Simply doing the right thing allowed Wentz to have a tremendous impact on Lukas and his family.

"We spent a lot of time talking about him while we were in the hospital," said Lukas' mother. "The idea of the hope of Carson Wentz and what it meant for the Eagles was another piece of inspiration for Lukas and his continued drive to get back on the field himself."

Lukas returned to the hospital, and one of the employees there passed on his story to the Eagles. Wentz recorded a message for Lukas.

"Hey, Lukas, Carson Wentz here. I know you're a big fan and made it out to a game last year," Wentz said in the message. "I just wanted you to know that we are all thinking about you. We wish you the best and God bless, bud."

As the cancer spread, representatives from the Make-A-Wish Foundation asked Lukas if he had a wish he'd like fulfilled. The one thing he wanted to do was thank Wentz for sending him the video.

The Eagles made arrangements for Lukas to visit the team at the NovaCare complex on May 30. That's when he got the chance to thank his favorite quarterback in person.

Lukas wanted to give Wentz one of his green "Dutch Destroyer" bracelets as a thank-you. From Wentz's perspective, all he wanted to do was take the boy's mind off the solemn situation that he was going through.

"I tried to just view it as an opportunity for Lukas to just take out all of the other stuff in his life," Wentz told ESPN. "The sick, the pain, the exhaustion, everything that he was going through. You could tell he was sick and that he was struggling, but he was a trooper that day."

Lukas had a great time at the facility. He got to meet many Eagles players but spent the most time with Wentz and his favorite defensive player, linebacker Jordan Hicks.

Lukas toured the facility as he spent the day with his favorite players. He even got to meet Eagles head coach Doug Pederson. It was a surreal moment for young Lukas.

Two weeks later, Lukas passed away. He was only 10 years old. Wentz wrote a letter to the Kusters family and sent it along with flowers that he had delivered to the funeral. The family had the handwritten letter framed, and it still serves as a connection to their son's favorite football player.

Simply doing the right thing allowed Wentz to have a tremendous impact on Lukas and his family. Lukas was buried with Wentz's jersey on. Wentz was moved to tears when he was told about it.

"It's crazy, to think that he was buried wearing my jersey," Wentz said as he fought back the tears. "It's so much deeper than

Wentz hugs Rebecca Burmeff, whom Wentz befriended during her son's fight with cancer, Monday, October 23, 2017, in Philadelphia. (AP Photo/Matt Rourke)

football. That's what it comes down to. It's more than just a game."

When Wentz took the field for the 2017–18 season opener, he had Lukas' bracelet on his wrist. Wentz said he hasn't taken the bracelet off since Lukas gave it to him.

"I feel Lukas all the time. It's always nice to just have him on my wrist," Wentz said. "It's a constant reminder that it's so much bigger than football. I have just been praying for that family. It's a very moving story, obviously. It's pretty cool to be in this position and make that impact."

Before a Monday Night Football game against the Washington Redskins in Week 7, Wentz met with Lukas' family and took pictures while the feature re-aired on ESPN's pregame show.

The second-year quarterback was delighted to give the family the ball from one of his touchdown passes. This one was after a pass to tight end Zach Ertz for a touchdown.

"I talked to them for a while. I saw them again after the game. Finally got the touchdown pass to Ertz and finally got the ball to them after the half," Wentz said during his postgame press conference. "They are just a special family. It has impacted me in a big way. I am just thrilled that they could be here. And the youngest one, that was his first Eagles game, so I told him he'd better keep coming back."

The story of Wentz and The Dutch Destroyer is just another example of how the young quarterback has a way of endearing himself to others. ★

Wentz talks to the relatives of Lukas Kusters, Monday, October 23, 2017, in Philadelphia. (AP Photo/Matt Rourke)

Wentz huddles with children during an NFL Play 60 event at Grant Park, Wednesday, April 27, 2016, in Chicago, before the 2016 NFL Draft. (AP Photo/Kiichiro Sato)

Suddenly an MVP

I n only his second season, Carson Wentz emerged as an MVP candidate by leading the Eagles to the best record in the NFL. Heading into Week 12 of the 2017–18 season, the Eagles were 9–1 and Wentz was leading the league with 25 touchdown passes.

"He improves every single week. The guys around him really elevate their game," head coach Doug Pederson said after Wentz threw four touchdown passes against the Broncos in Week 9. "I think we talk about this quite a bit with great quarterbacks and good quarterbacks that make the other guys really want to play at a high level."

The team is having fun and finding success with Wentz leading the way. Wentz earned the right to have a good time after the work that he's put in. He is always the first in the building and usually the last one to leave.

"He's doing a great job. He knows where everybody's going to be. He prepares so well each week. It's fun to watch him when things are really clicking like that and to see the guys having fun doing that," Pederson said.

Offensive coordinator Frank Reich said he's impressed by how he'll peek into the film room after he arrives

Wentz scrambles against the Arizona Cardinals, Sunday, October 8, 2017, in Philadelphia. The Eagles defeated the Cardinals 34-7. (Al Tielemans via AP)

at the NovaCare complex and see Wentz already settled in as he's studying the next opponent.

It's all about preparation. Wentz has a lot of freedom to change protections as well as the play before the ball is snapped. That freedom comes from a great deal of trust by Pederson.

Quarterbacks coach John DeFilippo works with Wentz every day. The success that Wentz has achieved is no surprise to DeFilippo.

"Carson is a guy that nothing surprises you because of the way that he prepares. The way he conducts himself on a day-to-day basis, the interaction with his teammates, his work. It's all detail-oriented," DeFilippo said before leaving for the bye week.

What is it that makes Wentz such an improved player this year?

"Just overall, he's seeing the field well. He's really getting comfortable with his teammates, the new guys on the team," DeFilippo explained. "Carson is throwing the ball on time and accurately. He's really stepped up in the leadership role and is truly a leader of this football team."

Recognition always comes when a player's team is winning. As the Eagles continued to add to their league-best record, Wentz's name was starting to be mentioned with Chiefs quarterback Alex Smith and Patriots quarterback Tom Brady as MVP candidates.

In fact, Wentz was the odds-on favorite to win the MVP award according to various gambling sites that accept prop bets.

Every week Wentz makes a play that leaves his teammates shaking their heads.

Sometimes it is a precise pass to a spot that no one besides the receiver can catch. On other weeks, it's an amazing escape from pass rushers that shocks his teammates.

Alshon Jeffery said his goal was to come to the Eagles and help make Wentz the MVP. Judging how things look so far, Jeffery's purpose is coming to fruition. The receiver has come to believe Wentz will wow him every time they take the field.

"That's what we expect," Jeffery explained after a 51–23 win over the Broncos in Week 9. "We expect him to make throws and great plays with his legs. All the credit goes to him."

Wentz has the Eagles on target for a deep run in the playoffs. He is among the league leaders in multiple passing categories.

What is so remarkable about Wentz is that he has taken skills that were marked for improvement and made them strengths. The great quarterbacks are able to throw their receivers open. That's especially the case on slants, dig routes, and dagger routes. Being able to throw to a window and lead the receiver requires accuracy. Wentz has made strides in that department on passes over the middle of the field.

Being able to accurately take deep shots is another area that Wentz got better with. He became a more precise deep-ball passer as the season went on.

The result is an Eagles offense that is nearly unstoppable. ★

LeGarrette Blount, left, and Wentz celebrate during the first half against the New York Giants, September 24, 2017, in Philadelphia. (AP Photo/Michael Perez, File)

Wentz celebrates his first NFL touchdown against the Green Bay Packers, Monday, November 28, 2016, in Philadelphia. (Jim Mahoney via AP)

Spreading It Around

Having an abundance of weapons on offense can be a double-edged sword for a football team. There is only one ball, after all, which means some players are not going to have it as much as they might like.

It takes a group of players that buy into the team-first mentality to make things work. Carson Wentz's steady, team-first attitude has played a crucial role in keeping everyone on the same page.

Everyone has to make a sacrifice, including Wentz, who does so when he breaks the pocket and dives head-first to finish a run. He puts his body on the line to get extra yards.

There are also times when Wentz hangs in the pocket for that extra second to give his receiver a chance to make his break as he releases the ball. Wentz has absorbed some major hits as he delivered the ball to his wideouts.

That doesn't go unnoticed. Philadelphia's receivers respect the reckless abandon that Wentz plays the game with. They understand that Wentz is going to throw the ball wherever his reads take him.

"Look at his athleticism, look at his inspiration to his teammates and how aggressive he is," former NFL quarterback Boomer Esiason said when asked about Wentz on *Inside the NFL*.

It is clear that Wentz is spreading the ball around to keep everyone involved. For the first time in team history, the Eagles have three different receivers with five or more touchdowns (Zach Ertz, Nelson Agholor, Alshon Jeffery) through nine games.

"Everybody is involved. A lot of that has to do with the play design that week," Eagles quarterbacks coach John DeFilippo said before the bye week. "We have so many guys that we can put in different spots. I think we

Wentz throws a pass against the Los Angeles Chargers, Sunday, October 1, 2017, in Carson, California. The Eagles defeated the Chargers 26–24. (Kevin Terrell via AP)

have a lot of versatile guys in this offense that can do a lot of things."

Offensive coordinator Frank Reich likens the Eagles offense to a basketball team. They have a lot of scorers, and Wentz is the point guard. He has to distribute the ball.

"It makes us hard to defend," Reich said at a press conference in October. "We don't have anybody averaging 30 points a game, but we've got five guys who can score. And so you don't know who it's going to be week to week, who can beat you, and I think right now that's what we're doing well. We have to play to that strength."

Wentz is a quarterback who is well ahead of the typical second-year player. Take his 59-yard touchdown pass to Torrey Smith against the Arizona Cardinals in Week 5, for example. Smith was running a route on the backside of the play in which he doesn't usually get the ball. Wentz adjusted his read to look Smith's way because of the coverage Arizona's defense presented.

"It was a post. I saw he was off and he was looking inside a little bit, so I just made sure I crossed his face and that no one was in the middle of the field," Smith explained after the game. "I know that on that play it never really goes there, but with that coverage, I know what [Wentz] is thinking and I was expecting it."

Seeing the field clearly allows Wentz to get the football to everyone. His vision is an underrated trait. Perhaps the best sign of his wide range of vision came against the Los Angeles Chargers. The play happened

Wentz directs the offense against the Arizona Cardinals, Sunday, October 8, 2017, in Philadelphia. (AP Photo/ Matt Rourke)

in the first quarter of their Week 4 game. Philadelphia had a play-action pass called and Wentz rolled out to his right side.

All of Wentz's reads were to his right, but somehow he managed to see LeGarrette Blount leak out of the backfield on the left. Wentz threw the ball across his body to the opposite side of the field.

It wasn't supposed to happen that way. In fact, Wentz's offensive coordinator would have used the play as a coaching point—if it wasn't for the 20-yard completion.

"That was one that you get in the film room with him and say, 'Don't ever do that again!'" Reich said. "That was a freakish play. That's not in the scramble rules, to scramble right and throw it back across the field."

"He's [Blount] there just in case the play breaks down, and Wentz has to scramble to the left. In no way should that ball have gone to LeGarrette," Reich said. "That was simply a case of a great player making a freakish play. I don't know how he even saw him. Just a great player making a great play."

Those kinds of plays are hardly a rare occurrence for Wentz. It's his way of carrying out the delicate task of making sure everyone is taken care of.

The fact that Philadelphia is winning is surely a factor in the team's ability to comfortably get everyone involved. However, a lot of the credit also goes to the Eagles' MVP, Carson Wentz. ★

Philadelphia Eagles wide receiver Torrey Smith (82) celebrates his touchdown with a baseball themed celebration that includes running back LaGarrette Blount (20) tight end Zach Ertz (86), Wentz, and wide receiver Alshon Jeffery (17) against the Arizona Cardinals, Sunday, October 8, 2017, in Philadelphia. The Eagles defeated the Cardinals 34-7. (Al Tielemans via AP)

Eagles fans carry a sign supporting Wentz in Week 1 of the regular season against the Cleveland Browns, Sunday, September 11, 2016, in Philadelphia. The Eagles won the game 29–10. (Paul Spinelli via AP)

Wentzylvania

Carson Wentz knew he was coming to a city that was starving for a winner when the Eagles selected him.

"They're passionate here. They hate losing," Wentz said about the fans during his first press conference as an Eagle. "I fit right in. I hate losing. I'm real passionate about the game, as well. I think that's the general consensus that I keep getting from this Philadelphia area."

Pennsylvania has taken to Wentz so much that people have started to name the Eastern part of the state after him. The name Wentzylvania gained national recognition during Wentz's rookie year.

Fans flocked to the open practices to get a look at Wentz, even though he was not a participant due to a rib injury. Big crowds gathered by the lowest part of the stadium to get autographs or just shake his hand as Wentz and the Eagles came off of the field after practice.

They chanted, "CAR-SON! CAR-SON!" The rookie quarterback was a glimmer of hope for a franchise that had been searching for someone to take them to the promised land.

The popularity of Wentzylvania grew after Wentz's tremendous start to his rookie season. His first game, a win over the Cleveland Browns, earned Wentz Pepsi NFL Rookie of the Week honors.

A road win over the Bears followed in Week 2. In Week 3, the roof was blown off as Philadelphia hosted the mighty Pittsburgh Steelers and beat them 34–3. Wentz completed 25-of-31 pass attempts for 301 yards and two touchdowns against the cross-state rivals.

The rookie quarterback had officially turned Pennsylvania into Wentzylvania with that win over the state's *other* team. Wentz garnered Pepsi NFL Rookie of the Week honors once again, making it his second time winning the award in the first three weeks of the season.

There was even a billboard that overlooked I-76 near Lincoln Financial Field that read, WELCOME TO WENTZYLVANIA. Everyone had to get their hands on Wentz

A Philadelphia Eagles fan holds up a sign in support of Wentz during the second half of a game against the Pittsburgh Steelers, Sunday, September 25, 2016, in Philadelphia. (AP Photo/Chris Szagola)

memorabilia. Wentz's jersey soared to the top of player jersey sales.

There were local companies that printed T-shirts with Wentz's image and the new name for the state emblazoned on them. One of the most successful ones launched soon after the Eagles' convincing win over the Steelers. That company was called Wentzylvania™ Clothing Co.

The creators were wise to strike while the iron was hot. Fans rushed to the company's website looking for merchandise. The reason for creating the company was simple.

"Now we see the man who can lead us out of the abyss," cofounder Jack Daddona Jr., of Allentown, Pennsylvania, told newswire. com. "Do we need to say his name? We all know who he is. He's No. 11, he's our guy, our franchise quarterback eading us to our destiny. So that's why we started our company. So that all of us could embrace him and take a little piece of destiny home."

Wentz's personality is a true match for Philadelphia. Known for his preparation and hard work, he has endeared himself to everyone from the members of the front office to his teammates and even the local media.

Executive VP Howie Roseman knew Wentz would thrive in a city like Philadelphia.

"When you talk about Carson, you're talking about a blue-collar quarterback," Roseman said during Wentz's rookie season. "He fits into this city, into the personality of this city, and you see that when he plays."

Wentz celebrates with fans after leading the Eagles to a 29–14 win over the Chicago Bears, Sunday, September 19, 2016, in Chicago. (AP Photo/Charles Rex Arbogast, File)

The popularity of Wentzylvania grew after Wentz's tremendous start to his rookie season. His first game, a win over the Cleveland Browns, earned Wentz Pepsi NFL Rookie of the Week honors.

"It's a blue-collar, hard-working-mentality city. That's how I am wired," Wentz told 94WIP during the bye week. "I am a blue-collar, hard-working kid who by the grace of God made it to this level. They are passionate about the game and so am I. It's great to be able to play in a city like this."

Head coach Doug Pederson was in Green Bay when the city fell in love with Packers quarterback Brett Favre. Pederson has compared Wentz to Favre because of their gunslinger mentality.

"You're seeing some of the same things that I saw in Brett in Carson: the toughness, the good, accurate throws, and eyes are down the field extending plays with his legs," Pederson explained. "Another thing that Brett was able to do, and you're seeing it with Carson, is just elevate the players around him."

Pederson didn't mention another similarity between the two: their "aw shucks" approach to things. No moment is ever too big for players like Favre and Wentz. Favre used to defuse tense situations by doing something silly, like asking for a "left-handed football" or imitating famous college football broadcaster Keith Jackson.

Wentz is the same way. He is able to laugh at himself, like the time he accidentally locked himself in a New Jersey bathroom before his rookie season.

Rarely is there a player who is so in sync with the city he plays for.

Given that the arrow is pointing up for the Eagles in only Wentz's second season, the love affair between the quarterback and Philadelphia should only continue to grow. Wentzylvania appears to be a place firmly planted on the map. ★

Wentz poses for a photograph with a fan during training camp, Friday, July 28, 2017. (AP Photo/Matt Rourke)

Wentz acknowledges a fan as he runs off the field after a game against the Washington Redskins, Monday, October 23, 2017, in Philadelphia. The Eagles won 34–24. (AP Photo/Matt Rourke)

Wentz holds up his jersey on stage after he is selected by the Eagles as the second overall pick during the 2016 NFL Draft, Thursday, April 28, 2016, in Chicago. (Ben Liebenberg via AP)